1979 BOYER LECTURES

Each year the ABC invites a prominent Australian to present the results of his or her work and thinking on major social, scientific or cultural issues in a series of radio talks known as the Boyer Lectures.

The series was inaugurated in 1959 under the title of the ABC Lectures, but in 1961 the ABC re-named the series as a memorial to the late Sir Richard Boyer. As Chairman of the ABC, Sir Richard had been one of those chiefly responsible for the introduction of the original series.

For my dear mother Edith,
who died during the preparation of these lectures,
and for my father, Clem

1979 BOYER LECTURES

THE RESOLUTION OF CONFLICT

RJL HAWKE

Published by
THE AUSTRALIAN BROADCASTING COMMISSION
145-153 Elizabeth Street, Sydney, NSW
Postal address GPO Box 487 Sydney 2001

Cover design by Susan Kinealy

National Library of Australia card number
and ISBN 0 642 97612 0

Price $2.50*

Typeset by Photoset Computer Service Pty Ltd

Printed in Australia by Hedges and Bell Pty Ltd
© Australian Broadcasting Commission, 1979

*Recommended price only

CONTENTS

INTRODUCTION

There is an advantage in writing this introduction after the actual delivery of the Boyer Lectures now incorporated in this book. It gives the opportunity to reflect upon some of the reaction to those lectures.

First, however, let me re-state my purpose.

For some time I have had a profound concern that our society and the world of which we are part are subject to forces of change so turbulent in character as to be fast constituting a condition of crisis. I have attempted in the Lectures to point up some of the resultant conflicts and to suggest some possible avenues for the resolution of these conflicts.

The ambitious nature of my theme 'The Resolution of Conflict' does not imply that these are more than suggested avenues; I make no claim to having definitive answers capable of meeting the complexities of the conflicts about which I speak. I have only one certainty and one hope — that we are in dangerous times and that my efforts may provoke thought and public debate on these issues.

To a considerable extent this has already begun and, for this, I am grateful to the media which I trust will continue actively to promote such discussion. Governments if they are to have the will and courage to act decisively require an informed and inquiring population — relevant mandates will only emerge from a concerned electorate.

I am deeply grateful to the great many people who have responded positively to the Lectures. Of course, there has been some predictable negative reaction from a few persons who appear to be totally content with things as they are. To them, and indeed to all readers, I merely say this: while change and adaptation of our attitudes will certainly pose some difficulties for us all, these will be as nothing compared with the potential chaos facing our society if we meander on enveloped in the warm cocoon of apathy spun from the threads of an earlier, easier and increasingly irrelevant age.

RJL HAWKE

HOW WE ARE GOVERNED 1

A series of lectures requires a title and a title requires explanation, certainly when that title is as apparently ambitious as 'The Resolution of Conflict'. Perhaps some clarity is first achieved by saying what I am *not* about. I am not advancing some general conceptualised theory about conflict and its resolution, nor is there an intention to talk about the resolution of conflict between individuals, an area of my own life where I have, at times, been less than spectacularly successful.

Rather, I have a very profound concern that we, both as Australians and as citizens of the wider world, are moving towards a condition in which the fundamental values of a free society will be at risk, and indeed the survival of civilisation in question. Our capacity to influence these global issues is minimal, but within the sensible recognition of those limits we should make our voice heard.

It is, however, very much, almost exclusively, within our own capacity to furnish ourselves better to handle the circumstances of crisis emerging within our own country. But we are participants in a paradox. We are daily witnesses to the fact and impact of change unparalleled in our memory, change which is being reflected in the structure of our economy, our capacity to provide employment and in the very cohesiveness of our society. And yet we are constitutionally and institutionally immobilised — in the framework for the conduct of our affairs, nothing changes. It is not change itself of which we should be afraid, it is this paradox of change/no change, the total lack of symmetry between our innovative capacities as technical and political human beings, that should cause us alarm.

9

These are the issues in my mind and I hope that the thoughts I wish to share with you in this context will not be seen to hang too uncomfortably upon this apparently ambitious peg.

My theme is the product of a tenuous optimism which I believe will only have validity if we are prepared to be thoroughly astringent in our thinking and debate with one another. We must be prepared to query the certitudes of our system; we must, whatever our predispositions, forsake resort to platitudes when these questions are asked; we must not assume that we are the unique occupants in the whole stream of human history of the perfect and unimprovable houseboat. It is in this broad sense that I wish to speak with you about the Resolution of Conflict.

With that broad explanation of title, may I briefly make five preliminary points. One, I assert the primacy of this theme — we are not experiencing, or are about to experience, a period of mere turbulence where some interests within society may be marginally disturbed. Of itself that should not concern us. What is in question is the very fabric of a free society. Two, I am very conscious of the honor extended to me by the ABC in being the first person actively involved in party politics to be asked to deliver these lectures. Identified as I have been as a spokesman for particular groupings, I have no intention or desire to pursue partisan purposes in accepting this honor. I believe, deeply, that all men and women of goodwill, whatever their political persuasion, should be responsive to the issues about which I wish to speak with you. In particular, I believe that any Australian Government, whatever its party composition, would be better able to serve the interests of our people if the changes which I advocate were to be accepted by the community. Three, I do not wish to be overly academic and full of learned references in what I have to say. We have had too much of elitism from those who would preach reform — if we are to have acceptable and constructive change in our society, it must emerge from discussion by a broad spectrum of our people of issues stated simply and debated with a minimum of rancour.

Four, and it follows from this, I do not claim all the suggestions I will be proposing in these Lectures are without difficulties. They are put forward precisely in this spirit: of hoping to promote such debate. Five, clearly I can make no claim to deal with all matters pertaining to this broad topic which I have chosen, or indeed to match the priorities in this respect of every listener. I have been extremely fortunate to have had the opportunity of experience and thought in a number of areas which I regard as extremely relevant to my theme — it is of these that I would now like to speak in more detail with you.

In any community the ultimate institution for the resolution of conflict between, and for the furtherance of the interests of, its citizens is the Government. The question must therefore be asked at the outset — how are we governed? Do we in Australia in the last part of the twentieth century have the structure and form of government best calculated to achieve those objectives? In response to the latter of these questions I believe the answer is clearly in the negative; and perhaps the best way of indicating why is to ask this question — what do we mean by 'we'?

In this world of some four billion people, are the 14.4 million who inhabit the geographical confines of a place on the map labelled Australia, New South Welshpersons, Victorians, Queenslanders, South Australians, West Australians, Tasmanians, Northern Territorians, and only in some residual sense Australians? Having been born in South Australia, educated in Western Australia and now lived in Victoria for twenty-one years, I have no feeling that my identity is to be found by some reference to lines drawn on a map defining the limits of those States. I am an Australian.

And yet those lines determine how we are governed.

Those lines, representing the meanderings of British explorers some one hundred and fifty years ago as they etched out a new colonial structure, still determine the present-day structure of Government in this country. Those lines determine that we must be surely the most over-governed country in the world — we have fourteen Houses of Parliament, one for every million of our population. For representatives of the six colonies, demarced by those lines, met in the three constitutional Conventions of 1891, 1897 and 1898. They met with a clear commitment to maintain the largest degree of legislative autonomy for the new States consistent with the cession of those powers necessary to enable the Government of the new Federation to discharge those functions perceived to be beyond the competence of the colonies acting separately. Some delegates had the grand longer-term vision of one nation, of one people, but the constitutional instrument finally fashioned out of the Conventions faithfully reflected this colonial commitment.

It was perfectly natural to expect this outcome, for it represented the realities of the experience of the delegates to the founding Conventions. They did not know one economy, but six. Their welfare had not been affected by common political circumstance but by the separate legislatures which they knew and of which most of them were members. What they knew was for them large, relevant and, not unimportantly, provided the opportunity of power. What they were creating — a federal legislature — was of limited and uncertain relevance, and should not be adorned with any authority which would unnecessarily diminish the functions and prestige of the institutions they understood, respected and enjoyed. This was, however, no dereliction of duty. The decision of our founding fathers did reflect, not merely their preferences and prejudices, but the reality of the economic, political and social influences which, until then, had determined the welfare of their respective constituencies.

All that was nearly one hundred years ago. The essential distribution of powers between State and Federal Governments embodied in the document emerging from the 1898 Convention has not been changed in that time. But the nation has changed almost beyond recognition. We are not, and have not been for a long time, six economies, but one. To use the language I have just employed, the reality is that overwhelmingly the economic influences determining the welfare of the people of Australia are either national in their dimensions or international in their origin and only capable of a sensible response by a national government equipped with appropriate constitutional authority. That authority does not exist.

The absurd folly of this position was given classic expression exactly twenty years ago in the *Report of the Joint Committee on Constitutional Review* established on an all-party basis by the Menzies Government. Let me quote from the most relevant passages of that *Report*:

Whilst the Founders were of one mind in allotting to the Commonwealth responsibility for defence which was, after all, a traditional function of government, there was, in their time, no acknowledged responsibility of governments for the general state of the economy. Consequently, no conscious effort was devoted to the powers needed to obtain and maintain a stable economy or to divide economic powers between the Commonwealth and the States. . .

Since the Constitution was written, it has become generally accepted that governments have a responsibility for the state of the economy. This is true, not only in Australia, but in all modern democratic countries.

In Australia it has become a recognised task of the Commonwealth and not the States to deal with matters which determine the climate of economic activity. One reason for this is the rapid growth of the economy since Federation.

Tremendous structural changes have occurred in Australian industry which have far outstripped the capacity of individual States to take effective action. For example, public companies exercise a significant influence on the general level of demand, especially for capital goods, and their spheres of activity increasingly tend to spread beyond the limits of one State. The impact of company activities on the economy may be such as to require regulation which must obviously be on a national basis in order to fit into the general pattern of economic policy.

. . . From the six separate colonial economies there has emerged, in the present century, a national integrated economy. Advances in transport and communications, the development of industries and specialised economic activities, the growth of the population, and numerous other factors, including internal ones, such as the establishment and development of markets for Australian goods overseas and the stimulus to industrial development resulting from two world wars, have tended to make the States inter-dependent, and, from an economic point of view, the Australian economy can only be regarded as a single unit. There has grown from the economic matrix contributed by the dissolution of separate State economies a most complex fabric of trade and business in which there is an inter-dependence between the many activities constituting the whole economy and between these activities and the climate of the economy as a whole.

. . . The economic history of Australia over the past fourteen years clearly shows how the forces at work have moulded Australia into a single economic unit and have made the Commonwealth responsible for the health of the economy.

. . . The Commonwealth has had to grapple with the broad problem of maintaining stability and promoting national development from a position of constitutional weakness. . . . The constitutional powers . . . fail to match the responsibility which the Commonwealth is called upon to discharge.[1]

That was true in 1959 — it is infinitely more true in 1979. For we are not talking about abstract hypothetical issues appropriate to a discussion between lawyers as to what would be a more elegant constitutional model than another. The perpetuation of this anachronistic lunacy is hurting Australians every day of every week.

It is most obvious to people who have to move about the country, whether they are travelling on business or on holiday, or are moving house because they have been posted to another State. If you are going by car, as soon as you cross the border most of the things you have to look for, change. The road signs are different. Probably the speed limits are different. The police force is different and the penalties for offences differ depending on your State of residence.

If you happen to be moving house and you have a family, the first thing you will find in your new State is that the educational system is different. You will find that the educational qualifications of your children are not necessarily accepted automatically in the new State, any more than they would be in a different country. Part of the children's education, especially at university or technical college level, may have to be repeated.

If you happen to get involved in legal proceedings with someone who lives in a different State, you will find that you have to deal with two different court systems. If your case happens to be in the family law area, you don't even need to cross a State border to get involved in two court systems; it is very likely that different aspects of your case will be dealt with by a Commonwealth and a State court.

Workers doing identical jobs in the same State, or in different States, can enjoy quite disparate rates of pay and conditions because they work under different State or Commonwealth awards.

Business men do not need to be reminded of the sometimes bewildering variety of rules, regulations and laws they have to comply with if their business crosses State lines, as so much does today. If you happen to be in the road transport business, you may quite often have the strange experience that the cheapest route is the longest way round. This is because, owing to a quirk of the constitution, at a time when we are all being urged to save petrol it is often cheaper to route a truck in such a way that it crosses a State border and comes back again, than to send it direct from one point to another inside one State.

The same constitutional provision, section 92, by making it very difficult for governments to ensure orderly marketing, directly affects the price paid by families for many food-stuffs.[2]

You may well ask as Australians, especially that one quarter of you who have come to join us from other countries and to whom this particular antipodean antiquity must seem almost totally incomprehensible, why and how we have continued to tolerate it? A good question. The answer, I think, is that we, who are by nature a fairly conservative people, have come to be infatuated by an assiduously cultivated phenomenon called 'States' Rights'.

I must confess that I do not have any idea what 'States' Rights' are. I do not understand, speaking as a person who happens to live within an area designated on the map of Australia as the State of Victoria, what 'rights' that State has. I understand that I, together with the other Australians who live in the same area, have rights, but I do not understand that an entity called the State of Victoria has any 'rights' independent of the sum of the rights of those people. I certainly do not comprehend that this entity has some 'rights' against another like entity called the State of New South Wales. And I am totally baffled when it is said that the State of Victoria, presumably speaking for me, has some 'rights' against the Commonwealth, presumably also speaking for me.

The truth, I think, is to be found in the power, prestige and opportunity for patronage that have accumulated within the operations of the States system. All political parties have come to acquire a vested interest in the perpetuation of this anachronism. On the side of business there is, at least in many quarters, a perception that there is less likelihood of effective intervention of the public interest in the conduct of its affairs in the absence of clear constitutional powers residing in the central government. In the trade union movement many leaders would see a greater possibility for pursuing the interests of their members in a system of competing State and Federal conciliation and arbitration jurisdictions.

And so what is, in reality, an attachment to the privileges of the States system by those who enjoy them is dressed up in the mystical language of 'States' Rights' as though such language is actually saying something meaningful about the interests of the people as a whole. I am not implying that there are no persons of integrity who operate in one way or another within this States system. Of course there are, and it would be patently ridiculous to argue otherwise. But it is even more ridiculous to perpetuate this myth about 'States' Rights'. Australians now live in an economic environment national in dimension, and their interests are predominantly determined by the capacity of government to deal with and improve that environment. In this sense the only significant way to talk about 'rights' is to assert the 'rights' of Australians to have these interests protected and advanced by a structure of government which is relevant to and capable of dealing with that environment. The nature of economic developments in Australia, and in the world of which we are part, since the time when we established that structure of government, has ensured that it now does not meet these critical criteria of relevance and capacity. Not only is the 'States' Rights' concept not positively relevant to our present economic realities, but worse, as we have seen, the continuation of an increasingly irrelevant structure creates very real impediments to the sensible conduct of our affairs. In the terms of the theme of these lectures, our present structure of government is not well calculated to best achieve a resolution of conflict; in fact, that very structure of government is itself a significant source of traditional and unproductive conflict within our community.

In a time of crisis, communities no less than individuals examine the apparatus which they have created to defend their interests — to see that they are in the best position to maximise the use of their resources to protect, and if possible to advance, those interests. This is a normal and intelligent response to the perception of crisis.

The crisis created by war is, of course, easy to perceive. The founding fathers gave the defence power to the Commonwealth in placitum (vi) of Section 51 of the Constitution,[3] and that power has been liberally interpreted, in war, to give the Commonwealth Parliament virtually unlimited power, particularly in the economic area, to deal with the crisis of war. By such interpretation the whole structure of the distribution of powers between Commonwealth and State Governments has been radically transformed, in such crisis, without resort to the complicated machinery of referendum, so that the resultant structure would match the realities of that crisis and of the economic environment and resources which had to be mobilised to meet that crisis. Put simply, the structure of Government embedded in our Constitution was recognised as irrelevant and inadequate to deal with the crisis, and placitum (vi) was, quite literally, the defence mechanism to release us from the folly of attempting to protect ourselves with such instruments — to save the structure we abandoned it.

But the interests of the Australian people are not put at risk only by the threat of war. In this respect I feel compelled to refer again to the *Report* of the all-party Joint Committee on Constitutional Review:

Twice since Federation there have been war-caused national crises. In two world wars the Commonwealth has had to undertake many tasks of government including the regulation of business activities, normally beyond its legislative powers. . .

National crises do not, however, arise only by reason of the threat of external aggression. Since the severe economic depression in the early 1930s, it has been only too plain that internal economic crises of a national character can occur affecting the welfare of every member of the community. It is the Committee's view that economic depressions, no less than war, may be national catastrophes. The rapid development of the post-war economy carries with it a continual threat of inflation which, if unrestrained, could have quite disastrous consequences. For that matter, a country in the throes of a chronic economic recession is generally weaker in world affairs and probably incurs a greater risk of being the victim of various types of aggression than at any other time. Yet as the Committee has pointed out, the Constitution does not vest general economic powers in the Commonwealth Parliament.[4]

Those words are unusually percipient, written as they were twenty years ago when the 'Lucky Country' syndrome prevailed, when the experience of full employment, low inflation and steady if unspectacular economic growth produced in most people complacency as to such constitutional issues. Those grounds for complacency have disintegrated and have left us facing a situation potentially warranting the term 'national catastrophe' used by the 1959 all-party committee.

We are delinquents to ourselves and our children if we do not move to meet this crisis with a more appropriate structure of government. If our society is to have any chance of dealing with the problems of growing unemployment, high inflation, depressed levels of economic activity, dramatic changes in technology and the pressures of developing countries for greater access to our markets — the elements of crisis — then we must have one government with the unquestioned powers to match the dimension of those elements.

There is no justification now, in terms of the interests and the rights of fourteen million Australians, to perpetuate this dangerous anachronism. What is unique about us that we need our fourteen Houses of Parliament and eight governments?

The vast size of our continent is sometimes advanced as a justification for the present structure. The very opposite is true. The ratio between small population and huge area means that the harnessing and harmonisation of this vast dispersion of people and resources poses greater problems of economic management than in most other countries in the world; in particular, the economics of transportation assumes a very special significance for Australia. And yet, more than almost any other country we tolerate the retention of the most unrealistic obstacles in the way of meeting these responsibilities.

I believe the logical implication of this analysis is that Australians would be better served by the elimination of the second tier of government — that is the States — which no longer serve their original purpose and act as a positive impediment to achieving good government in our current community. This would give us, like the great majority of other countries, one Parliament with powers available to the government to match the responsibilities upon it of protecting and advancing the interests of Australian citizens.

It would be desirable in these circumstances to strengthen what is now the third tier, local government, so that in relevantly demarced geographical areas people could participate in the decision-making process on issues appropriate to be decided at that level.

Of course this is a radical proposal, but we allow ourselves to be prisoners of history at the risk of the real deprivation of our rights and liberties in the future. Professor Colin Howard has put it well:

> The rigidity of our present structures derives in large part from a failure to perceive the true character of our national attitude towards constitutional amendment. In no other walk in life would such an attitude be tolerable for a moment. It amounts to an assumption that final wisdom was arrived at in the 1890s. We blandly ignore the twentieth century. Such an approach to life in any other context would be seen as self-evident folly. All that is different in the constitutional context is that the folly has become so entrenched and familiar as to seem part of the natural order of things.[5]

My proposal rests on the same conceptual basis as the 1959 all-party *Report* but goes beyond their recommendations because the history of the last twenty years compels a more rigorous logic. But the proposal is at one with that *Report* in being absolutely non-partisan. I seek by the proposal no advantage for any political group but for the people of Australia, by ensuring that any government of whatever political persuasion, when duly elected, shall have the powers which are relevant to the dimensions and structure of the issues determining the welfare of those people.

And when the defenders of the status quo throw up their hands in horror at the proposal, I ask my fellow-Australians to cut through the rhetoric, look at the arguments, and ask a simple question — how are my interests and those of my children advanced by this proliferation of ex-colonial governments those defenders would seek to maintain?

Finally, to help you answer that question, may I pick up an earlier point. If tomorrow Australia became involved in war, we would effectively abandon the present structure for the simple reason that it is a less efficient method of conducting our affairs as a nation. Why, at the time of greatest crisis in our peace-time history as a nation, does the logic of this escape us?

Notes
1 *Report of the Joint Committee on Constitutional Review* 1959 paras 1021, 1022, 1026, 1027, 1028, 1054, 1055
2 I am indebted to interchanges with Professor Colin Howard of Melbourne University Law School for stimulating my thoughts on the foregoing practical illustrations of the adverse impact of our anachronistic Constitution on the day to day lives of Australians.
3 Section 51. 'The Parliament shall, subject to this Constitution, have power to make laws for the peace, order and good government of the Commonwealth with respect to:
(vi) The naval and military defence of the Commonwealth and of the several States, and the control of the forces to execute and maintain the laws of the Commonwealth'
4 *Report of the Joint Committee on Constitutional Review* 1959, paras 1032, 1033
5 Howard, C *Australia's Constitution,* Harmondsworth, Penguin, 1978, pp162-3. Colin Howard is Hearn Professor of Law and Dean of the Faculty of Law at the University of Melbourne.

HOW WE ARE GOVERNED II

In the first lecture I have argued that we are still prisoners of our colonial history. I suggested that we are paying a very considerable price for our servitude in a structure of government less than ideally suited to the resolution of conflict and which, in fact, itself positively adds to the sources of conflict in our community.

I wish, in this lecture, to talk about the actual form of government in Australia and to suggest again that we are in this respect the prisoners of an even more ancient history. When the colonies achieved self-government they inherited the Westminster system, and it is that form of government which prevails at Federal and State levels in our country today. I find it inconceivable that a form of government which originated more than seven hundred years ago in an island off the coast of Europe is *necessarily* the best form of government for Australia as it moves towards the twenty-first century. Before good souls of British stock consume themselves in rage, let me make it clear that this is not said in disparagement of the achievements of the Westminster system, nor of the role it has played in the evolution of the democratic processes. Those achievements are unquestionable. What is questionable is whether a system which originated as a device to allow early kings of England to receive advice from, and resolve conflicts with, their barons and boroughs, and which has through time been adapted to meet changing circumstances, should not now be further adapted to make it a more effective instrument for the resolution of conflict within an increasingly complex society.

I want to make it clear that in what follows I am not here

arguing for a move to a presidential system of government. It is entirely possible to argue for an amendment of Westminster without arguing for either the presidential system or indeed entering the lists at all on behalf of those who believe we should become a Republic. The issues are quite separate. As far as the question of a Republic is concerned, I would merely offer the opinion in passing, that I do not believe Australians would essentially be any better off as a Republic, but for reasons of national identity I would prefer to break the link with the British Crown and have our own President as Head-of-State, possessing formal and ceremonial powers only.

As Professor Robert Parker has pointed out, the first essential part of the Westminster syndrome as it has developed to this point is the doctrine of ministerial responsibility, under which it is assumed that as much as possible of government administrative activity is brought under the direct control of elected ministers sitting in and 'responsible to' the parliament.[1] In answering the question of what, in this sense, is meant by 'responsibility', Parker indicates that the standard reply is: 'accountability — for what is done or proposed by the Minister or those under his authority — to parliament or the electorate, on pain of removal, voluntary or enforced, by the parliament or the electorate.'[2]

In other words, membership of either House of the Parliament is a necessary condition of participation in the Ministry and thereby the Government of the country. In our Constitution the requirement is formalised in Section 64:

> . . . After the first general election no Minister of State shall hold office for a longer period than three months unless he is or becomes a senator or a member of the House of Representatives.

I believe the time is overdue to ask ourselves whether Australia's best interests would not be served by amending this position. This is a radical proposal, but I suggest it does not make sense at this time to assume complacently that what has been 'good enough' in the past will suffice into the more difficult future. *The Economist,* in a leading article of November 5, 1977, reminded its readers that 372 years earlier Guy Fawkes had been discovered before he could blow Parliament up, and suggested he would be right to try again, this time to renew a democracy rather than a religion. In arguing trenchantly for reforms of the parliamentary system, *The Economist* referred to a growing cynicism about politics as such, and asserted that 'this cynicism is the canker in the body of British democracy itself'.[3] This same cynicism is increasingly evident in our own country and we are foolish to ignore it. We do not want another Guy Fawkes, but we certainly do need an honest preparedness to examine whether there are ways to improve the effectiveness, and therefore the image, of our system.

Two points appear to me of basic relevance. First, no-one, including the 188 senators and members of the House of Representatives themselves, would believe that the men and women with the best available administrative capacity for the government of the country repose exclusively in the two Houses of Parliament. Second, there is a considerable range of relevant and proven talent within the community which, while not desiring to be immersed in the party political electoral processes, would nevertheless be available and keen to serve the country in government.

If we are concerned with what is best for Australia, it seems we should then ask ourselves the question whether it is possible to 'marry' these facts into the Westminster system in a way which will maintain, perhaps strengthen, the doctrine of ministerial responsibility and, in the process, give us the opportunity of better government.

I believe that this can be done — I believe that it should be done, and these are my thoughts on how it could be done. Let me say, as a first observation, no-one is more conscious than I of our tendency to conservatism as a people, and of the need, therefore, for those who would advocate change to temper their fervor with a sense of gradualism. This constraint sits happily with me, and indeed I find considerable wisdom in the words of F S Oliver in his masterpiece on the life of Robert Walpole:

> In a changing world amendment is always needed; but anything in the nature of wholesale substitution would seem to be an act of suicide. The conventions may often seem absurd; but even these require to be treated tenderly; for real safeguards sometimes lie concealed within the most preposterous formulas.[4]

In this sense, I would advocate that as an initial step one-quarter of the positions in the Ministry should be open to be filled by persons not elected to the Parliament. Parliamentary elections would be conducted, as now, between rival parties going to the people with alternative policies, and the party or coalition of parties winning the majority of seats in the House of Representatives would form the Government. Given a Ministry of, let us say, twenty-eight it would then be open to the Government party through the Prime Minister, who would remain an elected member of the Parliament, to offer seven of those Ministerial positions to persons outside the Parliament.

These Ministers would not be members of the Parliament but would be responsible *to* Parliament in the following way: first, they would be present at Question Time to deal with questions concerning their portfolios; second, they would have ministerial responsibility to steer through the Parliament legislation concerning their departments, and third, similarly they would be required to be present for any debates concerning the handling of their portfolios or administration of their departments. In all these matters they would have the right to speak but not to vote.

In this way the important doctrine of ministerial responsibility to the Parliament would be maintained. It is, I believe, beyond argument that there are men and women of goodwill in industry, the professions, the community services, and the academic field who would be prepared, within such a framework, to offer their services for the better government of, and the better resolution of conflict within, our country. Such people would, I think, be equally available to both sides of politics without necessarily in either case fully embracing the total philosophy of the Government in which they were prepared to serve. They would be aware of the philosophy, and of their capacity to make their experience and expertise available in the light of their understanding of that philosophy. Such people would, I imagine, regard it not merely as a privilege but a duty to serve their country in this way. No side of politics could be disadvantaged; the whole body politic would be considerably improved.

Unless the proposal be seen just as some one-way stream of advantage being brought by those outside the Parliament, let some other words of Oliver remind you of the possible reverse benefits:

> If the critics came down into the mêlée they might lose some
> of their authority, but they would surely gain in sympathy
> and judgment. . . It might be for their souls' good, and also
> ultimately for the advantage of the cause they champion so
> disinterestedly if they took more part in the rough-and-
> tumble. For it is unreasonable to suppose that any section of
> these critics — least of all the idealists, the humanitarians, the
> pacifists and the magnates of the popular press — are at all
> lacking in natural benevolence: it is only that their humanity
> has been stunted by being grown in too small flower-pots.
> Were they released from their confinement, and planted out
> to take their chance in a free soil, from which the sourness is
> carried off by natural drainage, their virtues would probably
> flourish with as lively a vigour as do those of any politician.[5]

It is important not to perceive this proposal as an attack upon
those who become members of the Parliament under our
existing system. In fact the opposite is true and, as will be seen
from what I say later, I believe steps must be taken to enhance,
and make more effective, their strategic role in the good
government of our country. What is significant is that this
process of parliamentary election should not be seen as
exhaustively providing the pool of talent from which the
governmental administration of our affairs can be chosen. The
proposal to enlarge that pool by tapping the resources of the
whole community is entirely compatible with the maintenance
of the parliamentary system. Indeed, in some West European
parliamentary democracies, for instance Norway and the
Netherlands, all members of the Cabinet are precluded
constitutionally from being members of the Parliament, and
have a relationship with the Parliament of the type I am
advocating.

An additional advantage of the proposal is that the quality of
the Cabinet that a party could attract would become part of the
electorate's criteria in making judgment between the parties
seeking to form government. This very fact would through time,
I think, make all parties more acutely aware of public
aspirations as they engaged in their policy-making mechanisms.
Incidentally, it may also serve to produce what some would see
as a beneficial side effect of 'de-presidentialising' to some extent

our election campaigns.

While I have been arguing for a modification of the Westminster system in relation to the appointment of certain Ministers, it should not be assumed that the system has not already been drastically modified — some would argue, to the point of total departure from the basic concept. The doctrine of ministerial responsibility as originally conceived involved a two-way process — accountability of the Ministry to the Parliament *and* the obligation of the Parliament in turn to exercise a monitoring and surveillance function over the Ministry. Parliament fulfilled this function assiduously before the emergence of a strictly disciplined party system, which, however, both here and in the United Kingdom, has made a mockery of this two-way concept of responsibility.

We are very much indebted in this matter to the Clerk of the House of Representatives, Mr J A Pettifer, who from his unique vantage point takes us to the heart of the problem in a recently released discussion paper on parliamentary reform prepared at the suggestion of the Speaker, Sir Billie Snedden, earlier this year. The Clerk says:

> There is clear evidence that the House today is not seen by the public or, indeed, by Members themselves to be an effective monitor of executive activities. Nor is it.[6]

He quotes evidence from the United Kingdom that the balance of advantage in favour of the Government against the Parliament is so great as to be 'inimical to the proper working of our Parliamentary democracy', and then puts the Australian position with a stark clarity warranting quotation in full:

> Part of the problem which the House faces is inherent in the Westminster system itself. The Constitution ties the House to this system through Section 64. . .
>
> Thus, the Executive must be drawn from the legislature, be maintained in power by the support of the majority but at the same time be responsible to the legislature. The accountability of the Executive to the legislature has always been regarded as one of the strengths of the Westminster system and indeed when the system was conceived it worked well. But the coming of the party system with its requirements of strong party allegiance and discipline *has overwhelmed the Westminster system and destroyed its original*

checks and balances. What happens is that the Executive now looks for support to a majority of Members in the House who are of the same political mind as itself. Rigid enforcement of party policy by Whips and the possibility of the loss of party endorsement now ensure that the policy of the Executive when placed before the House as legislation is largely agreed to as a formality.

Whatever real questioning there is by Government Members of Government proposals must take place in the party room — certainly not on the floor of the House before public scrutiny. The lack of open discussion is rendered more serious because Executive proposals are very largely formulated by the Public Service and, under present arrangements, the proposals are often not subject to close analysis, public response, until finally implemented or enacted.[7]

Parliament I believe must be given the opportunity of resuming something of its constructive monitoring role in the governance of our affairs. No-one, I think, believes the end of the party system to be imminent — that we are about to witness a return to a Parliament composed of unattached free-thinking souls giving and retracting their loyalties to fortuitously assembled Cabinets of the likeliest talents in the land. Nor would this in any way be desirable or sensible. The attempt to reassert this positive role of the Parliament and to enlarge the opportunities for Members to immerse themselves more effectively in the legislative process must therefore be made within this reality.

Mr Pettifer's discussion paper, I believe, gives the beginning of the appropriate answer. He argues for the adoption within the House of Representatives of the system of Standing Committees developed over recent years in the Senate. Under this system, proposed legislation or other aspects of government administration would be examined in depth by the relevant committee composed of members from both sides of the House, and, on a motion of reference by the House, committees would have power to examine experts either from within or outside the Public Service and would also be entitled to call upon the presence of the Minister in charge of the legislation. The system of committees would not diminish the authority of the House, but, as the paper specifically indicates, their usefulness would be 'in the field of scrutiny, advice and disclosure, and in the facility they (would) provide in allowing other views, scientific, electoral or academic, to be brought to bear on a problem.'[8]

To facilitate this important function the committees should be provided with substantial qualified research staff. Experience would show that an enlarged membership of the House of Representatives may be necessary to optimise the functioning of the Standing Committee system and the House itself. There is no doubt that adoption of the system would improve the quality of legislation, enhance the role of the legislature and increase the satisfaction and sense of fulfilment of the legislators.

It would produce for the House of Representatives what has been the effect observed by the Clerk of the Senate in respect of the operation of the Standing Committee system in that Chamber since its introduction in 1970. Mr Odgers says:

The Senate's standing committee system has significantly strengthened the parliamentary system of government by providing opportunities and facilities for the more thorough consideration of public affairs and, by establishing formal channels of communication between the Senate and the electorate, has stimulated more public interest in decision-making.[9]

This proposal for the establishment of the Standing Committee system is, as I indicated, the *beginning* of the answer as to how to enhance the role of Parliament and the Parliamentarians. I believe there is another, associated step which, if taken, would go very far towards achieving this objective and improving the quality of government in this country. I refer to the use of the institution which operates under the misnomer of the Public Service.

I say misnomer because in a very real sense I believe the so-called 'public' service has become the private service of the Minister. This is not intended as any attack upon members of the Public Service. Indeed it is because I believe we have a very significant range of talent in this service that I am convinced we should make it more available for the public benefit by exposing members of the service more thoroughly to the processes of an extended parliamentary standing committee system.

Public Servants, of course, currently appear and give evidence before parliamentary committees, but there are very distinct limitations in practice upon the areas in which they can be subject to examination. In particular, committees cannot question public servants on departmental advice to Ministers concerning matters of policy. The relevant guidelines state that 'the Government does not see it being the role of the official to take policy positions or to answer questions . . . seeking evidence or identification of considerations leading to a Ministerial or Government decision or possible decision, unless those considerations have already been made public or the giving of evidence has been approved.'

I believe there is strong ground for supposing that the effectiveness of Parliament and the quality of Government would significantly improve if this inhibition were removed or at least substantially modified. Obviously, some categories of information warrant confidentiality, but as a general principle it would seem desirable that members of the Parliament in their capacity as members of the relevant standing committee should have the opportunity of analysing and questioning the advice behind the decisions they will be called upon to endorse in the legislature.

From my own experience in dealing with Ministers and their departmental advisers on issues of considerable national importance, I am absolutely certain that the public interest would have been much better served had standing committees of the Parliament been given the opportunity of examining those advisers. This would not involve trying either to make public servants apologists for Government policies, or capitalising on them as critics of such policies. It would simply mean that the Parliament would have the opportunity of putting itself in the best possible position to make judgments of substance about the proposals which the Executive calls upon it to pass into legislation.

While it may in the first instance be met with some discomfiture by Ministers, and indeed some public servants themselves, it should be understood there is nothing in the proposal which intrinsically offends the Westminster concepts. Enid Campbell, Professor of Law at Monash University, has put the position in these terms:

It could be argued that rather than undermining ministerial responsibility, the revelation of departmental advisings reinforces it by providing an essential basis for the Parliament to make a judgment on the Minister's culpability and liability to censure.

Acknowledging that officials would be far less disposed — at least in writing — to give advice frankly, fearlessly and impartially, Professor Campbell nevertheless concludes:

It is doubtful whether the fostering of direct and public accountability on the part of officials does any great violence to the principles underlying the Westminster system. After all, the precepts of ministerial responsibility represent just one of a variety of possible expedients for subjecting the exercise of public power to the superintendence and judgment of the people for whose benefit that power is meant to be employed.[10]

I believe Professor Campbell in this latter observation gets to the very nub of the concern I have been trying to express in this lecture. Government ultimately is about the exercise of power on behalf of the people, and politics is about acquiring and maintaining the right to exercise that power. Politics to some extent has become debased in our country, in part because of the perceptions people have of politicians, but also because the actual practice of Government has become too remote from them. Parliament does not provide the link to Government, for it has largely ceased to be, and is certainly not seen to be, an institution of 'superintendence and judgment' on behalf of the people over the exercise of power by the Government: it is perceived essentially as a rubber-stamp for the government of the day. Having no other discernible function, and certainly none which involves direct participation with interest groups in the community, parliamentary politics has become increasingly an object of derision.

This should be a matter of overwhelming concern to us. The standard and quality of life of every person in the country ultimately depends upon the standard and quality of politics and of our Government. If the community has a low esteem of the political process this fact of itself will diminish the capacity of government to resolve conflict and will indeed add to the possibility of conflict in the community.

We should all, therefore, have a vested interest in lifting the public perception of politics. The community will be better off if people can identify their welfare with an effective parliamentary process rather than treating the process with cynicism and scorn.

If the party system has reduced the effectiveness of Parliament in its traditional role of the monitor of the Executive, then good sense demands that we should accept this reality and seek methods to renew its authority in the interests of the people.

It is in this sense I have put forward the proposals in this lecture. I do not claim any certainty of prescription, and I acknowledge the difficulties and objections which can be raised to them. But I am certain of the diagnosis. People have become cynical about politics and this is unhealthy and dangerous for our body politic. I believe the creation of the option to augment the Cabinet from beyond the Parliament could improve the quality of government and would stimulate the interest and confidence of the public in the political process. I repeat that the proposal is in no sense directed at those who have chosen the electoral path to serve their country. They are deserving of more support, and this is precisely what an expanded Standing Committee system with appropriate powers to examine relevant public servants would provide: importantly, it would also provide a consistent opportunity to involve more representatives of community interests directly in the work of the parliamentary apparatus. The committees would provide a more creative atmosphere than the almost inevitable adversary climate of the House, and should ensure better informed debates when matters considered by the committees reach that Chamber.

In advancing the proposals I share the hope expressed in the prefatory note to Mr Pettifer's paper that they 'will promote thought and, ultimately, action towards making the Parliamentary institution a more efficient instrument in its role in the government of the country'. That objective is becoming increasingly important as our society moves further into conflict and crisis. It is of those developments that I wish to speak in some detail in the next lecture.

Notes

1 Professor R S Parker: 'The Public Service Inquiries and Responsible Government' in *Public Service Inquiries in Australia* (eds R F I Smith and Patrick Weller) University of Queensland Press, St Lucia, 1978, p351
2 Parker, R S, p351
3 *The Economist,* November 5, 1977, p13
4 Oliver, F S *The Endless Adventure* Vol 1, 1710-1727, AMS Press, New York, 1970, p108
5 Oliver, F S *The Endless Adventure* Vol 1, p105
6 Pettifer, J A Unpublished Mimeograph, House of Representatives, Canberra, 1979
7 Pettifer, J A
8 Pettifer, J A
9 Odgers, J R *Australian Senate Practice* (5th edn), AGPS Canberra, 1976, p486
10 Campbell, E 'Ministers, Public Servants and the Executive Branch' in *Labor and the Constitution 1972-75* (ed Gareth Evans) Heinemann, Melbourne 1977, pp155-6

AUSTRALIA IN CRISIS I

I have been arguing the case for contemplating change in the way we as an Australian society make provision for the government of our affairs. My plea has been based upon the fact that our society, in other directions, has been overwhelmed by change of dimensions almost beyond our comprehension. We can recognise from our own experience the force of the observation by the contemporary American thinker, Kenneth Boulding:

> The world of today is as different from the world in which I was born as that world was from Julius Caesar's. Almost as much has happened since I was born as happened before.[1]

Now, we have not been left unscathed by this torrent of change. Indeed, Australia stands poised on the threshold of the 1980s more divided within itself, more uncertain of the future, more prone to internal conflict, than at any other period in its history. I wish in this lecture to think and talk with you about some of those changes, the conflicts which they are generating, and to point perhaps towards some avenues which may assist in the resolution of those conflicts.

It is possible, I think, to identify two basic sources of conflict-creation in our recent history of change. I intend to deal separately with them, although, of course, there are inter-relationships between the two. One source is associated with economic change, the other with changes in social attitudes.

Looking first at the economic aspect, we do well to remind ourselves at the outset that almost exactly forty years ago on the outbreak of the Second World War, Australia, according to the admittedly inadequate statistics of the time, had an unemployment level of approximately ten per cent in a population of some seven million people. This represented an improvement from the depths of the Great Depression, when more than a quarter of the workforce was unemployed, but was in itself a reflection of the fact that Australia had never in its history since Federation experienced anything like full employment.

From 1939 we began the 'Lucky Country' syndrome. With most of our traditional sources of supply for a range of manufactured products cut off, and with the need to sustain our armed forces in their growing commitments, Australian secondary industry received an enormous impetus. We moved from unemployment to a position where women who traditionally had not contemplated full-time paid employment were recruited for a wide range of jobs in industry. In the short space of those years of war the country moved from the total experience of unemployment to the point of enshrining in White Paper and in legislation a national commitment to full employment.

The commitment of the law flourished into an economic reality, with Australia emerging from the war physically unravaged, with strengthened industry, a wider-based labor force, and the economies of Europe and Japan devastated by that war. Our rural industries boomed as those economies in their period of post-war reconstruction cried out for our wheat and wool and other primary products. In turn we started to absorb from those European countries hundreds of thousands of people who became part of one of the great immigration waves in history. These migrants became an essential element in the further expansion of our manufacturing industry which was built up behind the protective apparatus of tariffs and import licensing arrangements. Some idea of the dimension and significance of the immigration program to Australia may be gained from the following figures: since 1945 more than three and a half million permanent new arrivals have come to Australia from overseas. This has produced the quite remarkable fact that, according to our latest census of 1976, thirty-seven per cent, or more than one in three Australians, were themselves born overseas or are the children of parents, or a parent, born overseas. The proportion of our civilian labor force born overseas has risen dramatically from twelve per cent in 1947 to twenty-six per cent in 1977.

Through the whole of the period from World War Two until the early 1970s, with very minor exceptions, Australia was able to sustain a full-employment economy. Indeed, for most of the period there were more jobs available than people to fill them. This was accompanied by a remarkable, and yet not sufficiently comprehended, revolution in female participation rates in the workforce. The upward trend became apparent in the 1950s and again may be appreciated by these figures: in 1954, females constituted twenty-three per cent of the workforce, while the latest figure for August of this year is thirty-six per cent. Within those overall figures for female participation rates, the most dramatic feature has been in respect of married females, who have moved from constituting seven per cent of the workforce in 1954 to twenty-two per cent at the present time. Put another way, almost one in four of the Australian workforce is a married woman, compared with one in fourteen a generation ago. Over forty per cent of married women are now in the workforce.

While full employment was sustained until the early 1970s, very considerable structural changes were occurring in the employment shares of the various sectors of the economy in this period. Here some statistics are necessary. In 1950-51 the sectoral shares of the workforce were: Rural — fourteen per cent; Mining — two per cent; Manufacturing — twenty-nine per cent; Services — fifty-five per cent. By the end of the full-employment period in 1974, the proportion employed in Rural and Mining had halved, Manufacturing was down four per cent, while the Services sector had a correspondingly massive increase of fourteen per cent — up to sixty-nine per cent of the total workforce. Indeed, in absolute terms there was an increase in employment in the Services sector of one and three quarter million persons over this period.

I apologise for this outburst of statistics. However, it is vital to have this background if we are to understand the problems of the present and the future. In the post-war generation of full employment, as job opportunities continued to run down in the Rural sector and began to peak in Manufacturing, to the extent we thought about the issue at all we tended to assume there was an infinite elasticity in the Services sector to expand and take up the slack. And in a sense the figures justified that assumption.

But let us look at what has happened since the 1973-74 period. The sectoral trends of workforce shares have continued, with the Manufacturing sector having fallen to twenty-one per cent and the Services sector risen to seventy-one per cent. In absolute terms, between May of 1974 and 1979, 200 000 jobs have disappeared in Manufacturing while employment in the Services sector has risen by 170 000.

As distinct, however, from the early period, these latest movements have not been associated with the maintenance of full employment. The elasticity of the Services sector has not been infinite.

Let me, as dispassionately as is possible, put the unfolding unemployment situation before you. More statistics, I'm afraid. If we take the six-year period from August 1967 to 1973, we find that from a full-employment base in 1967 the employment growth rate exactly matched the increase in the workforce at 2.7 per cent per annum. In the six-year period from August 1973 to this year the annual employment growth rate at 0.7 per cent has been exactly half the 1.4 per cent annual growth rate in the workforce.

In terms of registered unemployed with the Commonwealth Employment Service this has meant an increase from 67 000 in 1973 to just under 400 000 or six per cent of the workforce at the present time — an increase of 488 per cent over the period, or an annual rate of increase of thirty-four per cent. In the same period there was the associated radical change from an equivalence of registrations to vacancies, to the position where now there are twenty-two persons registered as unemployed for every registered vacancy.

These figures by no means tell the whole story. During this period there has been a decline in the participation rates in the workforce reflecting the withdrawal of married women, students remaining at school, and persons retiring before they normally would have, had employment opportunities existed. These factors have been the subject of study by the Australian Bureau of Statistics, and when they are taken into account it is reasonable to put the figure of those who want to work but cannot get employment at something like three quarters of a million or ten per cent of the workforce; this estimate is supported not only by the fall in participation rates but by the fact that economic circumstances have precluded a continuation of the trend line of *growth* in participation rates which has previously existed.

Without overlooking the very real problems posed for older people, the most tragic feature of this unemployment picture concerns our young people. In August of this year something like one in five of our young people aged between fifteen and nineteen who wanted to work could not get a job. Those registered represented thirty-five per cent of the total registered unemployed, which figure increases to fity-six per cent if those in the twenty to twenty-four age group are added. The obscenity of the 'dole-bludger' syndrome as applied to these young people of fifteen to nineteen is perhaps best understood when it is realised that there are thirty-three such persons registered as unemployed for every vacancy registered for that group.

Before speaking of the conflicts which these factors are creating in our society, I must refer to another insufficiently comprehended development in the Australian employment scene — the rapid increase in part-time work. In 1970, part-time workers represented ten per cent of all persons employed — the proportion is now sixteen per cent. The movement has been particularly dramatic in the last five years. In the period August 1974 to 1979 there was an actual decline of 44 000 full-time jobs in Australia and an increase of 230 000 in those in part-time employment. This trend towards a greater use of part-time workers since 1974 has been most evident in the services sector but has occurred in all broad industry groups other than manufacturing. In August of this year, of the nearly one million part-time workers in this country, almost eighty per cent were female, and just over sixty per cent were married females, reflecting the fact that of all married females in employment, forty-four per cent were in part-time work.

And so, if you like, we have come full circle in forty years — ten per cent unemployment in 1939, something like ten per cent in 1979 who would like work and can't get it. But in 1939, ten per cent was nothing new. It was a point in a permanent pattern of unused human resources redeemed by the fact that it represented a return to something like the norm operating before the devastating thirty per cent of the great depression.

Today could not be more different. A generation and a half of our people, the first in history, had grown accustomed to an environment in which there was more work available than persons to perform it — the question for so many was not 'is there a job?' but 'which job?'. As I have indicated, an important element in the creation of that environment was the influx of millions of people from other countries. In the earlier days of this great program there were difficulties and occasional nastiness as we insular 'Aussies' sometimes looked askance at the newcomers; but as the doubts about the durability of the full employment phenomenon dissipated we came to appreciate the enriching influence of this great range of people upon so many facets of our life. The certainty in our minds that Australia had been good to them came to be matched by an understanding of how good they were for Australia. We were even able in this new climate of full employment to slough off with surprising equanimity the barren White Australia policy which had made us not only a physical but a political island in our own area of the world. Full employment was the cement that bound our society together, enabled us to face the challenges of a changing world and, to some extent, came to nurture a degree of compassion for the less privileged amongst us. That cement is crumbling, and as it crumbles we can discern the beginnings of fracture in our society. Indeed, it is not difficult to perceive the emergence of two societies — the employed and the unemployed — something akin to Disraeli's 'two nations'.

While the 'dole-bludger' syndrome is perhaps now not so blatantly present, there is nevertheless an insidious tendency to identify the unemployed as the architects of their own misfortune — to attribute to them some intrinsic inferiority either of character or intensity of purpose. We should derive no joy from this. In terms of the impact upon the personality and attitude of the unemployed person this implicit character assassination seems to be infinitely more devastating than the assessment of rationality involved in the 'dole-bludger' syndrome — ie at least what is being asserted in that syndrome is that the unemployed person has made a calculated decision of achieving relatively greater satisfaction from being on the dole than engaging in paid employment. Nothing is more likely than this character assassination to alienate the unemployed and cause them to call in question their own worth.

While there is abundant evidence showing a relationship, particularly among young people, between growing unemployment and an increase in the incidence of hard drugs, crime, suicide and other socially pathological phenomena, it is dangerous simply to assert a causal relationship in these matters. Some of the most detailed analysis in this area has been undertaken by Professor Harvey Brenner, of the Johns Hopkins University. On the basis of national and states data for the United States, and for England, Wales and Sweden, he concluded in 1976 that:

> Overall the data showed that the association between unemployment rates and all the pathological indices was statistically significant. Consistency was also shown in these relationships across age, sex and racial groups among different states and for three countries.

But Professor Brenner emphasised that this did 'not demonstrate causation. They only establish that certain factors vary in a similar pattern and appear to be statistically linked.'[2]

The actual conflicts within the unemployed person and potentially towards society at large are undoubtedly present and pose enormous dangers for our cohesiveness as a community. We should be careful not to transform the potential more certainly into actuality by ignoring the impact of unemployment upon the individual. In this respect I would like to share with you what I believe to be a most percipient view expressed in an as yet unpublished paper by a recently graduated social worker, Beth Thyer:

> It is how each individual deals with the experience of unemployment, of money worries, boredom, declining self-respect, and diminishing chances of another job, how the feelings of shock, optimism, pessimism and fatalism are translated into individual behaviour that will determine whether or not a negative social impact will follow.
>
> Pathological behaviour may be the reaction of some individuals to these experiences, but it by no means is a necessary or generalised response. The danger of irresponsible or unsubstantiated assertions is that possible behaviour arising out of the loss of income, and the feelings that accompany the psychological experience of individual

unemployment, are seen as causal of such pathological behaviour. The logical outcome of this false and simplistic perception is that each unemployed individual becomes the repository of antisocial tendencies and, as a group, a potential threat to society.[3]

I wish to say more on this in a moment, when speaking about the possible resolution of these potential conflicts, but at this point let me refer to the second strand of conflict-creation in our society — changes in social attitudes which have been occurring during this same period.

Without being exhaustive, what we may refer to as previous 'certitudes' about religion, marriage, sex, and the status of women have been increasingly questioned and, by many, repudiated. Our more highly educated and widely travelled community has become an increasingly sceptical one. The old certitudes have not been replaced by new, unless it is the embrace by many of some sort of nihilistic hedonism. In the area of status of women and Aborigines the formal process of accepting their equality as human beings has not been matched by the hard political and administrative decisions necessary to give effect to that acceptance; this fact, of itself, produces guilt and conflict within our society. These feelings are compounded in times of economic difficulties because there is a reduction in the perceived capacity to deal with some elements of these conflict situations by enlarged real expenditure programs.

I wish to spend a little more time speaking about the status of women, for I believe the actual and potential conflict in our society involved in this issue is immense and far from sufficiently comprehended. I confess to being a very slow and somewhat blinkered learner in this matter. I think the best introduction I can give to what I want to say is to quote from the work of the brilliant French thinker, Simone de Beauvoir. Writing in 1949, she said:

Woman has always been man's dependant, if not his slave; the two sexes have never shared the world in equality. And even today woman is heavily handicapped, though the position is beginning to change. Almost nowhere is her legal status the same as man's and frequently it is much to her disadvantage. Even when her rights are legally recognised in the abstract, long-standing custom prevents their expression

40

in the mores ... Legislators, priests, philosophers, writers and scientists have striven to show that the subordinate position of woman is willed in heaven and advantageous on earth ... men ... do not *postulate* woman as inferior, for today they are too thoroughly imbued with the ideal of democracy not to recognise all human beings as equal ... from woman's point of view I shall describe the world in which women must live; and thus we shall be able to envisage the difficulties in their way as, endeavouring to make their escape from the sphere hitherto assigned them, they aspire to full membership in the human race.[4]

Thirty years have certainly not removed the relevance of these perceptions — rather, that period has witnessed the focusing of the issues into a sharper perspective.

As I have pointed out, more than one-third of our workforce is comprised of women, and more than forty per cent of married women are now in paid employment, constituting almost a quarter of the total workforce. The economy and standards of living we know today would collapse if women were to withdraw to their pre-war rate of labor market participation.

This may be called employment emancipation, if you like, but in no way does it represent the achievement of equal status for women. The range of employment readily open to women is restricted because of discrimination built into our education system and the attitudes of some employers and trade unions. There is still the unstated but operative assumption that women are not entitled to equal opportunity because their place is, or ultimately should be, in the home.

A complex of guilt is generated by our ambivalence as a society on this issue. Many married women who are not in paid employment have some sense of inferiority in relation to their employed sisters. Many of those who are working and have children feel guilty about the inadequacy of the care available for their children while they are working. There is resentment in sections of the community that young people are unemployed while married women occupy available jobs — the implicit assumption being that women, particularly married women, have lesser rights than other people. There is a gross lack of proportion between their constitution of half the population and the number of positions of authority women hold in government, business, trade unions and other organisations of significance within the community.

In sum, the truth is that we luxuriate in the comfortable assertion that women enjoy equality. We have salved our consciences by eliminating the more obvious discriminations like unequal rates of pay for work of equal value. But, in fact, we have not eliminated the inheritance of the millennia that women are lesser beings, an inheritance which still manifests itself in a whole range of prejudice and other forms of discrimination. We are, as a society, more aware of this dichotomy between principle and practice, but the very awareness is a source of guilt and conflict between women and women, between women and men, and within men and women themselves.

So much for the easy part. In coming to speak about resolution, let me emphasise that I am not presuming to suggest that I have anything like definitive answers to the conflict situations I have been talking about. I wish merely to offer some thoughts which to an extent may be new, and at least useful in stimulating the first step in the process of resolution — that is objective discussion within our community in a framework of the acknowledged dimensions and dangers of these situations.

In the economic area, obviously there are conflicting arguments about which policies are more likely to produce higher levels of activity and employment. It is not appropriate to pursue those arguments here, except to assert that it should be common ground between all parties to aim at the restoration of full employment opportunities in this country.

The achievement of this aim is complicated by the two factors of technological change and the rapid economic expansion of the countries of East and South-East Asia — matters I will be referring to in more detail in my final lecture. The technological revolution has surged from manufacturing industry by way of microprocessors, automatic writing machines and electronic data transmission systems into the service industries. Overseas evidence shows that these developments, as they are increasingly applied in Australia, will severely limit traditional work opportunities in this sector, the expansion of which, as we have seen, has been so significant in our full employment experience. As we sell our mineral and rural products to the rapidly expanding economies of our area, they will demand greater access to our markets for an increasingly wide range of manufactured goods: this will in turn impose further constraints upon the capacity of our manufacturing sector even to sustain its present depleted employment levels.

There is an overwhelming need for a national understanding of the vast and potentially devastating nature of the problems created for us by these forces together with the escalating cost of energy. For this reason there should be a convening, by Government, of a national summit conference of major employer organisations, trade unions and other relevant bodies, where all the facts, analyses and forecasts are put on the table. This should not be an occasion for grandstanding or point-scoring, but for a rational, objective dissemination of factual material in an attempt to create a general understanding of the dimensions of the economic problems confronting our country. This understanding is an essential pre-condition for creating the greater degree of positive co-operation which will be necessary for us to meet these challenges and the conflict they are already generating.

I have been totally convinced for some time now that this step is crucial. Co-operation can only be the product of understanding; confrontation and conflict are the inevitable and disastrous alternatives.

I end on that plea. Next week I will look further at the possible resolution of the conflicts of which I have been speaking in this lecture, and in particular will spend some time examining the same issue in the field of industrial relations.

Notes
1 Boulding Kenneth, 'The Prospects of Economic Abundance'. Lecture, Nobel Conference, Gustavus Adolphus College, 1966
2 Professor H Brenner: 'Estimating the cost of national economic

policy; implications for mental and physical health and criminal aggression.' Study for the Joint Economic Committee of Congress, USA, 1976

3 Thyer, E E 'The Social Implications of Youth Unemployment' an unpublished paper prepared for the ACTU Social Welfare Research Unit, 1978

4 de Beauvoir, Simone *A History of Sex* originally published in France, 1949 under the title of *Le Deuxieme Sexe* (2 vols). First volume published as a Four Square Book in 1961 under the title, *A History of Sex* pp12, 17, 18, 22

AUSTRALIA IN CRISIS II

In my last lecture I spoke about two strands of conflict-creation in our society, the first relating to our changing economic and employment environment and the second to changes in social attitudes. I wish now to go further into a consideration of possible resolution of these conflicts, and also particularly of conflicts in the important area of industrial relations.

As part of our approach to the resolution of conflict emerging from our changing economic and employment environment we must thoroughly reappraise the whole concept of un-employment 'benefit'. As I have said elsewhere, the current concept and levels of benefit are still firmly based on the postwar assumption that full employment is the normal condition of our society. According to this assumption the derivation of income for people in that society is perceived in terms of their participation in the production processes. These processes, it has been assumed, operate to provide work for all, and therefore unemployment benefits should not and need not be too substantial because they exist to cope with those who don't want to work or are in transition between jobs.

The facts quite clearly show that the full employment assumption is not currently valid, and yet as a society we persist with a 'benefit' concept based upon the continued relevance of that assumption. The very word 'benefit' — the dictionary definition 'a kind deed, a favour, gift, advantage, profit, good' — itself reveals the nature of the assumption and the barren inhumanity of its continued application. While society cannot provide employment for its members, the pro-duction/work/income nexus has to be abandoned as a

45

justification for our present parsimony to the unemployed. An assumption cannot be used to justify making second-class citizens of those who are unfortunate enough to constitute the living proof of the inaccuracy of the assumption.

Virtually all discussion about restoring full employment concentrates upon the supply side of the jobs equation and the real difficulties of restoring the balance between this and the demand for jobs. We should, I think, give a little attention to the possibility of getting closer to balance by looking at the demand side.

An increasing number of people are finding satisfaction and fulfilment from what, for want of a better term, is referred to as 'the alternative life-style' — that is, it is alternative to that style which provides for sustenance and the means of employment through direct participation in the conventional production processes. We in the conventional community tend to be condescending, if not contemptuous, of the alternative community. At present the only formal relationship between the two communities is through the payment of the dole, a totally negative, even destructive, relationship.

It seems to me it would make considerable sense for us to examine whether we could not create a much more constructive relationship between the conventional society and those who would prefer to live in the alternative communities. We are, for instance, almost uniquely blessed with abundant resources of land in congenial environments. Instead of the negative expenditure on unemployment benefits, the conventional society could assist in the provision of land and facilities for alternative communities and so establish a positive and much more creative relationship between the two.

I realise the possible difficulties in giving effect to these thoughts. I am merely arguing that it would be sensible to examine these concepts in some depth. In this financial year we will be paying more than a billion dollars in unemployment benefits — a necessary but totally negative and corrosive outgoing. We are, I think, unwise not to explore the feasibility of whether there can be some forms of more constructive expenditure which can create more happiness and harmony and a closer balance between the supply of, and the demand for, conventional employment. In this respect I have a feeling that there are many older people who, for no reason of economic necessity, remain in the conventional workforce for fear of being regarded as second-class citizens if they were to opt into the alternative communities.

We would have to ensure that appropriate incentives were maintained for training and participation in the conventional production system which would still be preferred by, and provide the means of fulfilment for, the great majority of our people. I am quite certain that we in the established conventional community should not perceive a recognised and assisted minority alternative community as any threat. On the contrary it would be infinitely more likely to contribute to an harmonious society than the burgeoning of a disaffected body of unemployed to whom society pretends it has discharged its obligation by the signing of a dole cheque.

Perhaps I can best bring together the thrust of my thinking in this area by saying, as I have on another occasion, that the question is whether we can return to the unique postwar full-employment experience by some tinkering with present policies, or are we faced with fundamental changes which require fundamental reappraisal of many of our basic assumptions. I am certain the nature and rate of change of the forces operating within our society, and internationally, are such that it is an exercise in futility to imagine we are either experiencing some mere cyclical departure from full employment or that we will return to those halcyon days simply by the application of cosmetic Band-Aids.

We can't walk away from technology nor can we say to the world — 'Stop — we want to get off!'. As we said in the *Report of the Crawford Committee* in a passage which may bear a recognisable stamp:

It must be understood . . . that improved technology can carry with it the capacity to provide better standards of living and, in some areas, release from dull and unimaginative work. Australia is part of the world economy, and a refusal to operate with the most advanced plant and equipment would place more jobs under threat where international competition was a relevant factor . . .

These observations . . . are made with the knowledge that Australians generally continue to embrace the concepts of rising standards of living through the production process. Some, of course, question the current validity of these concepts, as is their right. While, however, the concepts remain acceptable to, and the basis of action for, the great majority in this country, Australia must accept their logical consequences.

We said, in this context, that if Australia could not readily return to an historical full-employment situation

there will be need for a re-examination of social attitudes to work patterns, education and training, and of society's concept of the work ethic itself. The adequacy of present means of sharing total income between those in and those out of work will have to be investigated.[1]

Now real commitment to such re-examination is the key to the resolution of the conflicts being generated by the economic developments I have spoken of with you. Those developments clearly have deep implications for the welfare of our society; unless we are all prepared seriously to question the relevance of our assumptions, derived from a different period, that welfare will be increasingly in jeopardy.

I believe a similar conclusion is to be drawn when thinking of the resolution of conflict emerging as a result of the changing social attitudes of which I spoke in the last lecture. Behavioural clocks will not be turned back, however much some would like to see a general return to what I have called the certitudes of the past. We need much more tolerance of attitudes genuinely held by groups or generations perceived to be out of kilter with our traditional mores. After all, there is room for disillusionment.

But the plea for tolerance is not a one-way street. Just as disturbing as the complacency of those who are content merely to live in the past is the strident negativism of those who seem unable to discern any virtue in that past or in the institutions which, for them, embody it. For instance, the cynical dismissal by such people of the organised churches seems to me to do considerably less than justice to the manifest attempts by those institutions to address themselves to the current problems of our society. The Australian Council of Churches has consistently involved itself, in financial and representational terms, with issues such as the environment, Aboriginal land rights, refugees, and the plight of the Third World. The Catholic bishops recently endorsed a publication *Beyond Unemployment* prepared for them by the Catholic Commission for Justice and Peace — whatever arguments may be advanced about some of the prescriptions in that document it is a marvellously compassionate and insightful analysis of the challenges posed for us by this new feature of our society.

In other words, no-one should assume he or his group is the sole repository of wisdom and rectitude. In most instances there is some real ground for the adoption by people of positions which to others seem unjustified or preposterous. And in most people there is, I believe, ultimately a desire for harmony rather than conflict — to understand this is to take the first step in the resolution of the conflict which is in fact diminishing our community.

In talking about conflict-creation in this area I spent some time dealing with the status of women. I believe that in speaking here of the resolution of conflict we must be quite astringent. The surest guarantee for continued conflict is to perpetuate the gulf between principle and practice which characterises our community today. We simply should not tolerate the hypocrisy of, on the one hand, proclaiming the equality of women with men and, on the other, denying that equality in so many aspects of our educational, economic, financial and social life.

Legislation to remove these barriers will not immediately, or even in one generation, remove the inherited prejudice of thousands of years. But such legislation is necessary if we are to do justice to half our population, remove a pervasive source of conflict, and stimulate real equality of opportunities in the functioning of our society.

In relation to married women we should be just as straightforward. If a woman sees her happiness and complete fulfilment in terms of the family home, this should be thoroughly respected; we should abhor any perverse discrimination which would attribute any inferior status to such women, who will continue to constitute a significant proportion of our community. For those women who wish, or feel it necessary, to engage in paid employment outside the home, we should regard it as an obligation upon society to ensure, either at the workplace or other acceptable locations, completely adequate child-care facilities as a matter of justice both to the

the mother and the child.

I would like to spend the rest of this lecture talking about conflict in the field of industrial relations, and its resolution. First, let me say that the usual tendency in discussions on this subject is to gauge the quality of the industrial relations climate simply in terms of the level of strikes. To establish just how simplistic this view is, let me quote from a person not normally identified as one of the more radical figures in our political history. Speaking in his then capacity as Attorney-General in the Bruce-Page Government, Mr Latham (subsequently Sir John Latham, Chief Justice of the High Court) said in 1927:

It is frequently said that the object of industrial legislation should be to promote peace in industry. A good deal depends on what is meant by that term. The absence of strikes and lock-outs is merely a negative ideal. It is a mistake to approach this subject merely from the point of view of endeavouring to avoid something, instead of trying to attain something. Industrial peace, if regarded merely as the absence of strikes and lock-outs, is but accidental and precarious. Viewed only from that angle, industrial peace is not sufficient. There must be vigorous and positive co-operation between employer and employee towards a definite object — the success of the particular industry and the well-being and contentment of the particular industry and the well-being and contentment of the community generally. With that spirit in industry, there will be less difficulty in reconciling conflicting interests.[2]

In endorsing this positive emphasis by Latham fifty years ago, it is impossible to avoid impinging some issues which are a matter of current controversy. In order, therefore, to establish a broader political and historical basis than my own beliefs for what we ought to have in mind when considering this subject today, I think it worth while to quote briefly some other things Mr Latham had to say in the House in that period. John Latham said, in that 1927 speech:

A great disservice is rendered to Australia by emphasizing such troubles, and by representing Australia as a land of constant strikes. We do our own country a grave injury by exaggerating the strikes which occur ... The industrial problem is one of the most complex in the world, because it involves the interests, desires, and aspirations, the daily life, and the livelihood of the people, and there can be no simple solution of it.

In the same speech Mr Latham said:

The overlapping of awards and industrial determinations is indefensible. It produces an incoherent and chaotic state of affairs. In some industries . . . the time and energy of their executives and considerable numbers of their personnel are engaged in dealing with difficulties that are factitious and artificial and should not exist.

One year later Mr Latham said to the House:

I hope I have now made it quite clear that the non-existence of penalties for strikes and lock-outs is not necessarily inconsistent with arbitration or any other system of industrial legislation. Systems exist all over the world without penal provisions upon strikes and lock-outs . . .[3]

I doubt if anything has happened to change the basic wisdom of what Latham said more than half a century ago. Strikes, of course, can be disruptive, can cause considerable inconvenience to a great many people beyond the immediate core of the dispute and, normally, the community as a whole would be better off without them. But, as Latham insisted, the industrial relationship is an exceedingly complex one, and usually the taking of direct or provocative action by one side or the other is a manifestation of conflict about issues beyond those immediately apparent in the dispute. This is why our own experience of recent times sustains Latham's strong assertions that the operation of penalties normally does not operate to prevent or settle such disputes. Particularly is this true when the armoury of weapons ranged against organisations of workers seeking to set what they perceive to be a fair price for their labor is not matched by a mechanism to regulate the prices of other goods and services in the market which determine their standard of living.

I believe the more positive approach which could lead to the resolution of much conflict in the industrial relations area can be considered under three categories. First, we should acknowledge, as did Latham, that the legal and institutional framework within which industrial relations are conducted in this country is itself productive of additional disputes. I have already argued that we would be better off without the conflicts of federation, and probably nowhere in our affairs is this more obvious than in the industrial field.

The classic illustration is provided by the now famous *Moore v Doyle* decision of the Federal Industrial Court in 1969.[4] Because of the different registration requirements under State and Federal industrial legislation, this case established that Federal unions must recognise the existence of three separate and distinct bodies: a) the Federal union registered under the Federal Conciliation and Arbitration Act, b) the State branch of the Federal union, and c) the State registered union — and that they must ensure that the affairs of the latter two are administered separately although in practical day-to-day terms they are one and the same entity. The fertile and almost endless source of conflict created for warring factions by this artificial position led the Industrial Court to observe that

the system as required to exist by state and federal legislation and as it has evolved under that legislation in practice is technical, productive of artificialities, and in urgent need of the attention of the law reformer.[5]

Since then there have been enquiries, and conferences between State and Federal ministers, but these have not led to a complementary legislative resolution of this problem. We should insist on this being achieved, as there is simply no justification for the community having foisted upon it the burden of factional intra-union disputes which are stimulated and facilitated by the existence of this Federal/State jurisdictional jungle.

Under this category we should also face up realistically to the fact that there are far too many unions in Australia — approximately three hundred at the last count. This is not good for those represented and it is certainly not in the best interests of the country. The existence of competing unions has been a continuing source of conflict, sometimes in critical areas of the economy. From the community viewpoint, demarcation disputes are uniformly disastrous and have nothing to recommend them. Instead of making it more difficult, as is the case at present, legislation should facilitate the process of amalgamation between unions, providing always that full opportunity is provided for members of the unions in question freely and secretly to record their votes on the proposal.

Second, I believe there is considerable room to lessen conflict by looking to ways to improve the actual conduct of industrial relations between the parties. My major suggestion in this respect is that top management should regard industrial relations as a priority area warranting their own interest and involvement. In my own experience I have so often witnessed disputes affecting the welfare of the whole community unnecessarily prolonged because the handling of the dispute on the side of management has been left to people without sufficient status and authority to make decisions in negotiations. It has always struck me as surprising that management would never dream of divorcing itself from the decision-making process about major investment programs; and yet the efficiency, and profitability, of such programs can be significantly influenced by the outcome of negotiations on industrial disputes with their employees. To my present knowledge, one of Australia's major companies, a multi-national in its own right, has no industrial relations department. The managing director and the general manager assume responsibility with down-the-line management for the conduct of this company's affairs, and in the result it has one of the best dispute-free records in the country.

Perhaps, still under this category, I may be permitted, on the basis of some little experience in these matters, to offer just a few guidelines to parties in their conduct of negotiations in an industrial dispute situation. I think there are three main criteria which, if adhered to, maximise the opportunities of honorably resolving conflict. These are: one, a full and detailed preparation of the claims and positions to be adopted in negotiations; two, honesty about one's own position and a sense of reality in terms of understanding the position of the other side; and three, flexibility as the negotiating procedures unfold. I have witnessed so many damaging industrial conflicts which could have been either avoided or drastically curtailed if these principles had been followed by both sides.

A third category offers hope of helping to resolve conflict in our industrial relations. I refer to the concept of industrial democracy, by which is meant, essentially, the idea of encouraging a greater degree of involvement by employees in the affairs of their workplace. The argument in favour of this concept is based upon the view that in the production process society should distinguish between the inputs of materials and labor. We have long ago accepted the implications of political democracy — that is, that individuals should have a voice in the determination of their political destiny. This is justified by most of us in moral terms, and by those who are, by nature, of a more Socratic disposition it is rationalised by the belief that at least it ensures a greater measure of acceptance of the decisions by the elected leadership — however far those decisions may in fact be remote from the mandate of the election.

We seem to have been remarkably slow in applying the logic of either of these views to the position of people in the working environment. Men and women have rights in their industrial, just as in their political, personality, and the denial of the one will ultimately, I believe, prove to be as fraught with danger for our society as the denial of the other.

What I am suggesting should not be construed as some massive assault upon what are termed management prerogatives. The reactions of the extreme right are just as unreal as those of the extreme left, who picture industrial democracy, in our society, as a form of economic adultery on the part of the workers. Both positions are equally alien to the mainstream of Australian thinking.

I believe that management and unions should undertake the positive exercise of examining how, on a mutually acceptable basis, employees can be brought more into the processes involving decisions about their work program, conditions and environment — factors which determine to such an extent their opportunity for satisfaction in this community. There is no case for some uniform code of industrial democracy; each enterprise should evolve what is most appropriate to the experience and context of its own operations. So conceived, an emerging program of industrial democracy could help to resolve conflict in the Australian industrial relations scene and positively add to our economic performance.

I have talked with you in these four lectures about conflict and its possible resolution within Australia. In my final lecture I would like to speak about the international aspects of this theme, and then, if I can, draw together the many strands that have been worrying me and, I hope, interesting you.

Notes
1 *Report,* Study Group on Structural Adjustment, March 1979, chaired by Sir John Crawford, p14
2 *Hansard,* House of Representatives, December 15, 1927, Vol 117, p3276
3 *Hansard,* House of Representatives, December 15, 1927, Vol 117, pp3278-3279 and June 5, 1928, Vol 119, p5472
4 *Moore v Doyle* (1969) 15 Federal Law Reports, p59
5 *Moore v Doyle* (1969) 15 FLR at p123

THE INTERNATIONAL CONTEXT

In the first four lectures, I have been talking about aspects of conflict in Australia and their possible resolution. In most of the matters I have traversed there is obviously room for argument and strongly diverging points of view. But on one point there can be *no* argument. All our endeavours to create a better and more harmonious society in this country will have been a monumental exercise in futility if the world blows itself apart as a result of the failure to resolve conflict between nations or groups of nations. If that awesome bell tolls, it will have tolled for us.

Let me repeat what I said at the beginning of the first lecture — our capacity to influence these global issues is minimal. Our fourteen million people represent about one-third of one per cent of the world's population and will be an even smaller proportion by the end of this century.

This very fact, however, makes it imperative for us to recognise the forces of change and sources of conflict within our world which are operating today and are likely to be with us for the rest of this century. We should attempt to understand these factors so we can appropriately fashion our internal decisions and act in international councils in a way relevant to this changing global environment which will shape the destiny of future generations of Australians.

As with our own country, we can best begin to comprehend the possible dimension and direction of future change in the international arena by appreciating the magnitude of what has occurred from the time of the Second World War, a cataclysm which irreversibly altered the course of world history. A starting point to this understanding is provided by an observation in a recently released OECD publication, *Interfutures: Facing the Future.*

> When the invasion of Poland began, 80% of the earth's land areas and 75% of the world's population were controlled by the West as it then was, while 25% of each belonged to the British Empire.[1]

When that war was ending, the delegates of the fifty countries meeting in San Francisco in 1945 knew they were drawing up a United Nations Charter for a different world; none of them, however, would have foreseen just how different that world would become in the next thirty-five years as a result of the geopolitical forces which had been unleashed by the recent conflict.

Under the pressure of these forces the old colonial structure disappeared and the proliferation of new States has trebled the membership of the United Nations. Of the 152 countries now members of that organisation, 119 belong to what is designated the Third World. The Report recently submitted to the Australian Government by the Harries' committee — 'Australia and the Third World' — underlined the significance of this grouping:

> Taken together, Third World countries account for about half the world's land area, about half its total population and around 17 per cent of its total production. They supply approximately 90 per cent of world oil exports and 32 per cent of world exports in non-fuel ores and minerals. They include in their number countries ... which are middle-ranging military powers, possessing substantial and in some cases very sophisticated arsenals. If determined to do so, some Third World countries would be able to deploy nuclear weapons within a few years. Third World countries control access to canals, straits, waterways, bases, ports, airspace and airports which if denied could weaken the defences of the Western powers and affect adversely their economic prosperity. In some instances, such action by one or several Third World countries would produce an unfavourable and direct effect on Australia's strategic environment and economic prosperity. .... relatively small groups of Third World countries have the capacity, through changes in their international alignment, to alter profoundly the strategic

balance between the West and the Soviet Union and its allies.[2]

This analysis, of course, does not assume that the Third World is some homogeneous entity. Their common achievement of national independence is reflected in a general consensus of Third World countries on such issues as colonialism, racism and concepts of a new international economic order within the various organs of the United Nations. But in demographic and economic terms these countries have quite differentiated experiences and likely growth paths which of themselves will be a possible cause of future conflict.

In the period from 1945 the *increase* in population of all Third World countries more than equalled the developed world's present population of approximately one billion. It is estimated that by the end of this century, of a world population of some six billion people, about sixty per cent will live in Third World countries, or eighty per cent if China is included for these purposes; by that time seventy per cent of the total population of the Third World, so defined, will live in eight countries — China, India, Indonesia, Brazil, Bangladesh, Pakistan, Nigeria and Mexico.

Economic growth rates have ranged from negative to well above the average of three per cent for the Third World as a whole and, as the *Interfutures* document points out,

per capita incomes in the Third World range from $110, at 1974-76 prices, in Bangladesh, through $610 in Ivory Coast, $2,700 in Singapore, $6,300 in Libya to $15,000 in Kuwait. [3]

The evidence suggests that these disparities within the Third World in growth and per capita income will widen into the future with several Third World countries (in addition to the oil exporters) achieving, by the year 2000, income standards similar to those of some developed countries at the present time. It should perhaps be of some interest to us that on current projections Singapore is likely by then to have a higher per capita Gross National Product than Australia.

At the other end of the scale, poverty is currently a prevailing characteristic of the Third World. According to World Bank estimates, 800 million, or forty per cent of the Third World's two billion people — or in other words a number equivalent to the total population of all OECD countries — exist in conditions of 'absolute poverty'; and that level is only expected to fall significantly by the end of the century, on the basis of the more optimistic economic and demographic projections.

Clearly, there is not sufficient time in this lecture to elaborate adequately on *all* the significant aspects of the changes which are occurring in what I have referred to as our global environment. I have tried briefly just to give you some conception of the massive nature of these changes. What I hope I have succeeded in doing is to show just how futile it will be for us to imagine that we fourteen million Australians can proceed into the future upon some insular assumptions derived from a distant past.

To give point to this warning, let me dwell for a short time upon some features of these changes which are of immediate relevance to us. Our trading patterns have already changed dramatically in the past generation. As we observed in the Crawford Report, we have moved from a position twenty-five years ago when the United Kingdom took more than one-third of our exports and provided nearly one-half of our imports, to a point where that country takes only one-twentieth of our exports and provides only one-tenth of our imports. Japan has become our dominant trading partner, taking more than a third of our exports and providing more than a fifth of our imports. The eight market economies of South-East and East Asia, that is the five ASEAN countries: Indonesia, Malaysia, Singapore, Thailand and the Philippines — together with Taiwan, Hong Kong and South Korea — include the fastest-growing economies in the world and will, on present trends, within a matter of less than five years be as significant in world trade as Japan is today.[4]

These countries have married the latest technology to relatively low wage rates and are producing an increasingly wide range of sophisticated manufactured goods; in fact almost half of all the Third World's exports of industrial production comes from four countries in this area — Hong Kong, Taiwan, South Korea and Singapore.

As we seek to export to the countries of this area our minerals and rural products and, hopefully, specialised manufactured products of our own, we will have to provide greater access to this increasing range of their manufactured products. This will be a challenge containing sources of external and internal conflict but it is not one Australia will be able to ignore. I remind you that we have attempted in the Crawford Report to point the way to the possible resolution of these conflicts, by urging the adoption of an industrial adaptation policy which would (a) encourage the emergence of a more competitive manufacturing sector (b) promote flexibility and adaptability in the economy and (c) ease the adverse consequences of adjustment.

Any discussion about the future international context is obviously incomplete without reference to China, a country included in the Third World for some purposes but properly to be considered in a separate category. The inevitable importance of a country of some 900 million people has assumed an increased significance with the radical change of direction adopted by the Chinese leadership in February 1978 in its commitment to the program of economic development referred to as the 'Four Modernisations' — agriculture, industry, science and technology, and defence. There was some suggestion early this year, sparked by references to possible suspensions of certain negotiations with the Japanese, that this commitment was substantially in question.

I believe it is not, for the very simple reason that there will be no significant locus of power within China which will wish to divert the basic thrust of this policy. The armed forces will certainly want to see a strong and expanding economy, as will the potential élites in the educational, technical and professional fields who can perceive a more fulfilling and rewarding role in the massive infrastructure required to give effect to the four modernisations. And there is clearly no shortage of enthusiasm on the part of Japan and the Western powers to be associated with the program. There will, of course, be modifications, but the concept and course are irreversible.

This has important economic implications for Australia, which already has substantial trade with China. But I believe the issue of longer-term significance is the nature of the developing relationship between China and Japan. Japan last year enjoyed one-quarter of China's overseas trade; under the long-term Trade Agreement between the two countries updated in March of this year, two-way trade will increase enormously in the period to 1990, with the possibility that the value of each country's exports to the other could total $US30 billion between now and that time.

I believe that Chinese pressure for the supply of military equipment will be one of a number of influences leading in time to a resurrection of the heavy armaments industry in Japan and a significant growth in the defence forces of that country. This belief does not of itself involve any value judgment about such developments, but I suggest that such a possibility is relevant to any assessment of potential conflict in the rest of this century.

Certainly, the Soviet Union, which professes considerable cynicism about the capacity of China to achieve the targets of the new economic development program, is nevertheless deeply concerned at this intermeshing of the Sino-Japanese economies. Senior spokesmen for the Soviet have specifically expressed the view that this co-operation could last perhaps twenty years but that conflict would arise when Japan decided to become the third thermo-nuclear power. The relevant point for us is not the accuracy or otherwise of these prophecies but rather that we should not allow our thinking about the future to be entirely determined by comfortable assumptions as to what we would expect or like to happen in that time scale.

Although the world has avoided the ultimate disaster of the nuclear holocaust, war has in fact been the constant concomitant of our affairs since 1945. And for most of that period no area has been watched by the world with more consistent apprehension than the Middle East. The Arab-Israeli conflict has erupted into war on four occasions since 1948; and, because of the violent emotions involved and the energy imperatives which increasingly dominate the thinking of nations, it remains a major threat to the peace of the world.

For that reason and because, as you know, I have a particular interest in this area, I would like to talk briefly about this issue, particularly as I do believe there is a possible way through what appears to be a virtual stalemate, and it does seem to be one where it is perfectly appropriate for Australia to take an initiative, given our good standing with the countries directly involved and with the United States. In this discussion I, of course, put to one side, with contempt, those extremists who conceive of only one resolution of this conflict — the obliteration of the State of Israel.

While there are several difficult aspects, the critical question in the current negotiations is the future status of the West Bank. It is quite clear that President Sadat (and probably President Carter) have a quite different view to Prime Minister Begin as to what is meant by the documentation which emerged from and followed the Camp David summit in September 1978. The agreement provided for a one-year negotiating period between Israel and Egypt (and hopefully Jordan). The two relevant and related passages are to be found *first* in the joint letter of Sadat and Begin to President Carter dated March 25, 1979:

> The two governments agree ... that the objective of the negotiations is the establishment of the self-governing authority in the West Bank and Gaza in order to provide full autonomy to the inhabitants ...

and *second* in paragraph 1(c) of the *Framework for Peace in the Middle East Agreed at Camp David* (September 17, 1978) which says:

> When the self-governing authority in the West Bank and Gaza is established and inaugurated, the transitional period of 5 years will begin. As soon as possible, but not later than the 3rd year after the beginning of the transitional period, negotiations will take place to determine the final status of the West Bank and Gaza ... The solution resulting from the negotiations must also recognise the legitimate rights of the Palestinian people and their just requirements ...

Sadat argues that these words allow for the emergence of a separate Palestinian State, a proposition resisted by Begin. On this point I find it impossible to disagree with what was said by Aharon Yariv — Israel's military negotiator at Kilometre 101 after the 1973 Yom Kippur war — in an article in the *Jerusalem Post* on March 30 of this year:

> Without a doubt, different and conflicting interpretations of this paragraph can lead to serious difficulties between Israel and Egypt as well as between Israel and the United States. We should be realistic and recognise that autonomy, whether we like it or not, carries the seed of a Palestinian political entity.

But the basic and totally understandable Israeli fear is that the creation of an independent Palestinian entity on their immediate border would provide a strategic launching pad for an attack upon Israel and thereby threaten the very viability of the State. Egypt and the United States (together with a number of remote and comfortably placed armchair strategists) assert that this is a groundless apprehension. And this is the sticking point.

The realities are apparent — the reality of a Palestinian aspiration, the reality of Israel's fear, the reality of the Egyptian and American belief that guarantees can be provided to prevent the realisation of this fear. The question is — how to translate those realities into an acceptable settlement?

I believe this could be done in the following way. As Israel is assured that the new entity will not be used as a base for an attack upon her, a term is inserted into the treaty giving substance to that assurance by providing that should this in fact occur and Israel be forced as a result into war, then any new territorial lines emerging from such a conflict are non-negotiable.

The virtues of such a proposal are: *first* the aspirations of the Palestinians for their own separate entity are satisfied (as in fact they could have been at any stage for the nineteen years between 1948 and 1967 when the territories in question were under Arab and not Israeli control), and *second,* Israel is not left with a mere guarantee that it will not be attacked — which, in the light of their experience since 1948 and the existing PLO Charter calling for the destruction of Israel would, to the Israelis, seem somewhat less than convincing. In sum, if the assurances to Israel are sincere, those giving them should have no difficulty in agreeing to such a provision and would have every incentive to see that the assurances were in fact respected; for its part, Israel, if the assurances were broken, would have to defend itself, as in the past, but would do so in the knowledge that it would not subsequently be subject again to interminable international pressure on the crucial question of the security and recognition of its borders.

Complementary provisions would be necessary to cover any dispute as to whether an attack was in fact pre-emptive in character as was the case with Israel in 1967. This issue, I suggest, could be dealt with by the two sides agreeing in advance upon a panel of countries to be incorporated in the treaty, whose responsibility it would be to make a decision in the event of any such dispute.

Israel may well argue that the risk in these proposals is unconscionably high. I would like to comment upon that possibility by repeating some observations I made in April 1979. These remarks are, I believe, relevant not only to the precise subject of which I have just been speaking, but to other considerations which are at this time in the forefront of our minds; indeed, in some respects they capture very much of what I wish to convey generally of the need for new, bold and imaginative thinking about issues which can, literally, be a matter of life and death for us all:

> The agreements between Egypt and Israel have helped to dispel the illusion of hopelessness which had overwhelmed many men and women of goodwill around the world on this issue of the Middle East. The pattern of recurrent and increasingly devastating war had seemed to them irreversible. And despair is rarely a useful handmaiden to decent policy-makers or opinion-formers. These historic events have shown that there can be 'another way' than conflagration and death — that the crucible of war *can* be replaced by the councils of peace.

> The overwhelmingly important question is what will be the longer-term course of action of the other Arab States and the PLO in response to the treaty, both in relation to Israel and Egypt — and also in relation to the economic stability of the rest of the world. Short of war, as previously experienced, these States (and Iran) have it within their capacity to create continuing turmoil.

> The United States, Western Europe, Japan and their major trading partners are increasingly vulnerable in relation to Middle East oil. The United States is now importing 8.8 million barrels of oil per day (forty-six per cent of its needs) — some 2.3 million of these are from Arab producers, with more than one million a day from Saudi Arabia alone. And in strategic terms it should be remembered that the eastern end of Oman commands the Strait of Hormuz, through which passes between sixty-five and seventy per cent of Western Europe's imported oil, ninety per cent of Japan's and thirty per cent of America's. And the Strait of Hormuz is susceptible

to blockade.

In this context the position of Saudi Arabia is of crucial importance, and the evidence in that respect is not reassuring. On March 31, 1979, Saudi Arabia decided to support the Arab boycott of Egypt formulated at the Baghdad conference. How far, in fact, Saudi Arabia will go down that road is not yet certain, but without doubt this is one of the biggest question-marks over the whole future course of events in the Middle East, as indeed is the very question of whether the present regime survives or is moved to one more squarely in line with the Rejectionist Front . . .

In these processes of peace there are, and will be heroes, just as surely as there are in times of war. And just as there are risks in war, so there are risks in these processes of peace. The heroes will be those who see and know the risks and are prepared to face them . . .

The great *achievement* of recent times is that Israel has been recognised by the major Arab State. The great *task* of the immediate future is to ensure that this recognition is explicitly embraced by all other protagonists. The great *challenge* then for Israel will be to accept the reality of that recognition. Justice demands that these things go together — Israel cannot be expected to accept the one without the other.

Those thoughts, expressed in April 1979, seem to me even more valid today.

Apart from the Arab-Israeli question I have not specifically talked about avenues for the resolution of international conflict. My main concern has been to promote an understanding of the fact that we are part of a surging, unparalleled torrent of change in the world's history. To believe that we can isolate ourselves from the waves of that torrent would make Canute look like a calculating realist. Peoples have come to experience that political structures and divisions of power are not immutable. Nor will they perceive the distribution of wealth and resources between nations to be unalterably ordained in heaven and incapable of drastic rearrangement by the less than gentle manipulation of man. It is right and, to put the matter in the lowest possible denominator, it is in our self-interest, that Australia should join with other developed nations to accelerate the flow of appropriate assistance and technology to less privileged communities — and what is appropriate should not be left to the unfettered discretion of transnational corporations whose interests are by no means necessarily identical with those of such communities.

In this matter of our international relations and the diversion of resources it is a sad commentary upon our global community that the *Interfutures* document is able to make this stark comment:

> The overall figures for military expenditure are simply stupefying: the annual military budget of all the nations of the world is in the region of $US350 billion in 1976 terms — an amount equivalent to the annual gross product of the poorest half of the world population.[5]

Through history the factor that has consolidated previously warring tribes or groups has been the appearance of some common external threat — perhaps we do need a signal that the Martians are coming.

But now, if I can, let me in conclusion try to bring together the threads of these last five lectures.

Our country and our world are in this turmoil of change. There are many aspects of that change about which we can do nothing, and many which indeed we should welcome. But much of this change, unless properly understood and sensibly handled, has the capacity to diminish or destroy the environment within which the freedom of the human spirit may flourish. And there are forces which would feed upon these changes to achieve precisely that result.

More and more of our people, especially the young and underprivileged, will be increasingly susceptible to the blandishments of these forces if we do not provide them with employment or security with a sense of fulfilment. If we do not do this we have no right to demand or expect their adherence to the values of a free society.

Countries, and individuals, when threatened with the forces of change and conflict have the option of withdrawing into an isolationist shell, putting up the barriers of their own material achievements and hoping those forces will dissipate or pass by leaving them unscathed. This 'I'm all right, Jack' syndrome is morally bankrupt and strategically barren. There is an alternative.

We have a magnificent country — land, unlimited natural resources, and a fine people enriched by one of the great migration waves of history. We have the capacity to do justice to all those people, and through the sensible utilisation of those human and natural resources to make a significant contribution to the welfare of those beyond our shores who are considerably less fortunate than ourselves.

However, we totally delude ourselves if we imagine these things will happen by a mindless adherence to past assumptions or a blind belief in the adequacy of existing structures and attitudes to meet these volcanic forces of change. The world will not wait for us.

Let me say again, finally, that I make no claim to certainty for the prescriptions I have advanced for some paths to the resolution of the conflicts we face. If I have, in any way, stimulated you to engage in the greatest adventure of all — to think new thoughts — I rest content.

Notes

1 *Interfutures:Facing the Future,* The Organisation for Economic Co-operation and Development (1979), p66
2 'Australia and the Third World', Report of the Committee on Australia's Relations With the Third World. (Chaired by Prof. Owen Harries) September 1979, p14
3 *Interfutures,* p72
4 Report, Study Group on Structural Adjustment, Chaired by Sir John Crawford, Chapter 9
5 *Interfutures,* p376

OTHER BOYER LECTURES ARE:

1959 — *SOCIETY IN THE SPACE AGE, by Dr David Forbes Martyn, Chief Officer of the Upper Atmosphere Section of the CSIRO.*

1960 — *LAW AND POLICY IN THE QUEST FOR SURVIVAL, by Professor Julius Stone, Challis Professor of International Law and Jurisprudence at the University of Sydney.*

1961 — *THE CROWDING WORLD, by Professor WD Borrie, Professor of Demography, Research School of Social Sciences, Australian National University.*

1962 — *IN DEFENCE OF THE COMMON MAN, by Professor WGK Duncan, Professor of History and Political Science, University of Adelaide.*

1963 — *AUSTRALIA AND FOREIGN POLICY, by Professor JDB Miller, Professor of International Relations at the Australian National University.*

1964 — *ALONG THE EDGE OF PEACE, by George Ivan Smith, Personal Representative of the United Nations Secretary-General of East and Central Asia.*

1965 — *THE BRAIN AND THE PERSON*, by *Professor Sir John Eccles, FRS.*

1966 — *BIOLOGY AND THE APPRECIATION OF LIFE*, by *Sir Macfarlane Burnet, President of the Australian Academy of Science.*

1967 — *ARTIFICAL AUSTRALIA*, by *Robin Boyd, a leading Australian architect.*

* 1968 — *AFTER THE DREAMING*, by *Professor WEH Stanner, Professor of Anthropology and Sociology, Institute of Advanced Studies, Australian National University.*

* 1969 — *THE PRIVATE MAN*, by *Professor Zelman Cowen.*

* 1970 — *THE FRAGILE PATTERN*, by *Dr HC Coombs.*

* 1971 — *LIFE AND HEALTH IN AUSTRALIA*, by *Professor BS Hetzel, Foundation Professor of Social and Preventative Medicine, Monash University.*

* 1972 — *THE CHALLENGE OF CHANGE*, by *Professor Dexter Dunphy, Professor of Business Administration and Head of the Department of Behavioral Science at the University of NSW.*

* 1973 — *TODAY, YESTERDAY AND TOMORROW*, by *Professor Sir Keith Hancock, Emeritus Professor, Research School of Social Sciences, Australian National University.*

* 1974 — *HOUSING AND GOVERNMENT*, by *Hugh Stretton.*

* 1975 — *THE WEB OF CRIMINAL LAW, by The Honourable Justice Mitchell, CBE, Supreme Court, South Australia.*

**1976 — *A DISCOVERY OF AUSTRALIA, Manning Clark, Emeritus Professor of History at the ANU and one of Australia's most eminent historians, looks at the factors which have helped shape our history, and at his own development as an historian.*

**1977 — *WRITERS OF THE BULLETIN, by Douglas Stewart, for twenty years Literary Editor of The Sydney Bulletin.*

**1978 — *NATURE'S DEFENCES: New Frontiers in Vaccine Research, by Sir Gustav Nossal. The distinguished medical scientist looks at the importance of modern immunology in contemporary medical science.*

* These titles are still in print and can be bought at ABC offices. Please address inquiries to ABC Merchandising, GPO Box 487, Sydney, 2001.

**Also available as cassettes.